REALISTIC GUIDE TO STARTING AN ONLINE STORE

Taurius litvinavicius

CONTENTS

INTRODUCTION

This book was designed to get you started with online store business in a realistic way, therefore, if you expect to invest nothing and have high gains in thirty days – this book may not be for you. Ideally, you should be planning your investment on the interval of between five and twenty thousand dollars. Instead of telling you to do everything yourself, this book teaches you how to delegate. Therefore, some investment will surely be required.

We will begin with some basic terminology, to get you started, this is important, for some words might be intimidating, but once you learn them they become quite easy to use and read. After that we will take a look at a timeline you should have to setup your business and what will the options be to set up the actual store. Once you know these basics, we will dive deeper into the products. You will not be told which products to pick specifically, because many things may sell, but rather you will learn how to pick them and what to avoid. Coverage on the unavoidable marketing is also included in the book and it is also explained in a very realistic way, with no empty promises. Finally, you will learn a bit about upkeep, how to account for that and not get carried away. Then we will try to put everything together and create a little example plan.

Although not necessary, you should have some basic skills on MS Excel, you will see some examples in the book and once you are done - you will need to use.

BASICS

Profits, revenues, margins and statistics

PROFITS AND REVENUES

In any field, revenues and profits are the key elements of the business. In the most basic terms, profit is cost subtracted from revenue and revenue is every sale – all the money that came in.

$P = R - C$

> C for cost
> R for revenue
> P for profit

But what are these profits and what are these costs? In general, there will be two types of profits – gross and net, the net can also be divided into two parts – net before tax and net after tax. The cost is basically your expense on the product, it is not the price, the price is what the customer pays. For example:

Product cost = 40

Product price = 60

Profit on the product (gross profit) = 60 – 40 = 20

In this case, you would buy the product from a wholesaler for 40 and sell it for 60 and that is the price the   customer   sees.

MARGINS

This one word will impact your business a lot and it can get quite intimidating. But, the whole idea is acctually quite simply, a margin is simple the difference, the difference value. So, let us take a look at a few examples here.

R (revenue) = 100
C (cost) = 50

P (profit) = R − C = 100 − 50 = 50

Profit margin = 50 (P) / 100 (R) * 100 = 50 %

As you can see, in this case the profit margin, is the percentage value of the whole amount. So, it is the difference between cost and revenue in percentages.

P (price) = 100

S (shipping cost) = 20

C (cost) = 50

Shipping margin = 20 (S) / 100 (P) * 100 = 20%

This example shows the calculation of shipping margin, as you can see, it now a part of a structure, you have cost, your retailers. The margin in this case is that shipping part of the whole value.

STATISTICAL TERMINOLOGY

Although your plan should be straightforward, you will likely still need to use some fancier words. More importantly, you will surely need to understand them, during your research and on other occasions.

Let us start with some advertising and with the **cost-per-click**, also known as **CPC.** This is simply the amount of money you pay on average for each click. The example below shows how it would typically be calculated.

Total spent (T) = $100
Clicks (C) = 200 units
Cost-per-click (CPC) = T / C
CPC = $0.5

Normally, on advertising platforms you would also pay for views (impressions), so the actual calculation would be different. Although, there are alternatives and you will learn more about those in the marketing section.

Next, the **Conversion rate** – this metric shows how many clicks converted into customers or orders. The calculation is again, quite simple, you take all your clicks and divide them by the number of users who actually made an order after clicking your link.

Then, we get to the **click through rate**, also known as CTR. This may sound similar to conversion rate, but they are completely different, although can go along quite well. This metric requires the amount of impressions and the number of clicks, the result is quite simply the percentage of impressions that converted to clicks.

Finally, we get to the **cost per mile** or **CPM.** This one is probably the most popular and it measures the money spend for a thousand views (impressions) of your advert.

Impressions – views (I) = 15 000

Total paid (TP) = $15

CPM = TP / I * 1000

CPM = $1

As you can see from the formula, you simply have cost per single impressions, which is then represented as per thousand impressions. Since otherwise the number would be terribly small and difficult to read – per mile implementation is implemented. Kind of like Kg instead of g (kilogram instead of gram – 1000g = 1kg).

GENERAL

Timeline and development

TIMELINE

Before you begin anything, you need to set yourself a timeline, from initial plan and fundraising to the release of the platform. It should be clear and simple, but always remember – your goal is to get your business started, not follow some plan to exact point.

First, be realistic about it – understand how much time you have. Are you going at it full-time or half-time, or weekend-time, or maybe even couple-hours-a-week-time? If you have very little time yourself and not a wide budget, find the points where you will need to do several things at once and get help for those tasks.

In any project plan, you will have some tasks that can only be completed before others are. Having said, you should not forget one part of a plan for a long period of time. To achieve that, you can establish reviews of your plan every some period of time.

DEVELOPMENT OPTIONS

In general, you have three ways to get your platform developed. The first is to not develop it, simply use a solution like Shopify. The second option is to use various templates, themes and plugins. And finally, you can get your platform developed from scratch. All of them have their own advantages and disadvantages, from first to third will be cheapest to most expensive and vice-versa most scalable and least scalable. So now, we will get into some more details on these three options.

Using a platform that simply allows you to register and get started may sound very accessible and easy. And, of course, there is no upfront cost. But there is indeed a monthly cost, there is very little control on features and in general, you never know if they will not go under. But if you do decide to take the easy road, you will be paying a monthly fee and with that, additional fees for additional (premium) features.

Getting the store developed by someone who uses lots of plug-ins, add-ins, templates and libraries is a fine choice. It might be on the slow side and it will look like millions of others, but it will work. Also, customizing it should be relatively simple.

If you do have some money to spend, you can thing about hiring a real developer and having a site developed from scratch. This option should only be used when you have something custom, something unsual, otherwise it will be a waste of money.

PRODUCTS

Themes, prices and more

CHOOSE A THEME

Every store has a theme unless it is a general store, which you do not want to do, for the competition is simply unbeatable. So, what does it mean to choose a theme? The main thing you have to theme is your products, obviously, along that you may have a design theme, perhaps even one that matches the theme for your products.

To make it simple, you can choose from two options – pick a single product (product line), make your own product line or theme by category. The first option is quite straightforward, so let us explore the second one further. Your category should be quite lean, simply because you will not be able to sustain a large one. Take for example "Electronics" – that could be computers, keyboards, washing machines, kettles. So, instead of doing electronics, do "kitchen appliances", do "computer accessories". You see, each category can have more than one sub-category and that should be your theme.

You want to choose something you are familiar with, ideally at least. Have you worked in electronics store? Then choose electronics related theme. If you have worked with women's wallets, then choose that. In case you are not familiar with anything you should look for a category that has a lot of data online and you could get a good understanding about it with very little effort.

SET PRICES

Setting prices is one of the most important tasks, but doing that can be quite difficult, because where do you begin? The answer to that is quite simple, first of all, traditionally – the retail margin is about 50 %, but let us take a look at a few examples and some options on how to do it.

Here we have a table, which will allow you to experiment with the margin size, to find the best possible price.

	E	F	G	H	I
4		cost	margin	price	price (incl. vat)
5	p1	$ 34.56	50%	$ 69.12	$ 83.64
6	p2	$ 35.78	50%	$ 71.56	$ 86.59
7	p3	$ 37.00	40%	$ 61.67	$ 74.62
8	p4	$ 38.22	60%	$ 95.55	$ 115.62
9	p5	$ 29.44	50%	$ 58.88	$ 71.24
10	p6	$ 10.66	50%	$ 21.32	$ 25.80

	M	N
4	vat	21%

H5 function = F5/(100%-G5) *drag down*

I5 function = H5+H5*N4 *drag down*

As you can see, the VAT is added as a separate price, because it should not be calculated as a cost or an expense.

INITIAL ORDER

Whilst initial order is often treated as something you would just "give a shot", that is a wrong way to think about it. Remember, chances are, and high ones they are, that most of your initial stock will not sell. So, if you fail to determine the right amounts, you will be left with lots of useless stock and a bankruptcy on your hands.

You should always look at the minimum amounts and if your budget is not tight, do not spend more than 10 % of it for the initial order, it is better to sell out than throw away. As mentioned before, it is a good idea to have several products and with that, try to have less stock of products that are the most expensive. You can test the expensive products, whilst filling the stock with the cheaper ones. By doing that, you get a chance to test more products, but at the same time your store is not empty.

SHIPPING

When it comes to shipping, you will have two types of issues – pricing and logistics. No matter what you do, your shipping prices must be transparent and "shipping included" may not be the best thing for beginners. With that, you will get into logistics and whilst it may be a logistics horror, but if you take time to setup, it will be a pure pleasure.

Your shipping strategy should have several variables, not only the time it takes to deliver, but also several providers. The optimum number would be three providers – two couriers and one postal service. This will allow some choice for the user, in terms of brand they use and in terms of time it takes to deliver.

The good thing about shipping these days, is the fact that third-party systems are terribly easy to integrate. They will tell you what labels to put on, how to prepare something for shipping, so the only thing you will need to do is give it to the courier. You can go with UPS, DHL or whatever system you prefer, but do go with one that is popular and has tremendous resources all over the world.

WHAT TO AVOID?

Whilst nobody can really tell you what to sell, someone can tell you what not to sell. In fact, some products may be common sense, but some may be a bit trickier. This brings us to the topic of what not to sell and we have a list.

First, you should try to avoid anything that has a duty on. This would be tobacco products, alcohol, more to that point, this is more about the paperwork and licenses, rather than the tax itself. If you are importing something, it is quite likely you will pay a tax, but some products simply require a terrible amount of paperwork to take in and then take out as well.

The second bad option is cosmetics, with that – fragrances. Beauty products is a very competitive market and they most of the time they have a fragile expiry date. Although the possible high margin for the products may be attractive, avoid them as much as possible. The market is crowded with products, brands and stores that sell them. Choosing a good one is terribly difficult and even if you find a good product, it is likely it will not survive for long.

This one should be obvious and that is anything edible, from health and safety to licencing – there is simply nothing worst than selling food. On the other hand, if you know someone who sells some niche packaged products, you might want to give it a shot. But even with tight packaging, it is likely you will have lots of bureaucracy.

Finally, medicinal products – that is anything from drugs, to medical devices. Simply too risky and not worth the trouble. Just like the cosmetics, the margin will be quite high, but the risk is insane. First, you will need to deal with all kind of permits and then you are not even sure if it will sell, perhaps the product does not work, perhaps it has too many side-effects or perhaps there is a cheaper option? Too many questions, where answers are too expensive.

TIP OF THE SECTION

Theme your store, this is not about using the same fonts, colours and struct, although you should do that too. This, however, is about theming the selection in your store, theming your products. You cannot sell fragrance and food, you cannot sell shoes and computers. Or maybe you can? The important thing is for all the products to go together and for the store to have a theme. This could be hunting (outwear, sprays etc.), gaming (joysticks, keyboards etc.). In general, the store should be straightforward and easy to understand what you will find in it.

MARKETING

Discounts, advertising and more

SEO

Whilst SEO can be useful, it can also be useless. There's no question that you need a proper layout for the site, but there is no need to spend thousands on SEO.

No matter what you choose to do with the SEO, you need to have a good layout for the website, so that the links would have previews and other similar features would exist. Besides that, you should leave the SEO be until you have made some sales and therefore have some data to research.

DISCOUNTS

Just as many other numbers, discounts are rather difficult to create. One of the ways to do it, is to look at three stages of a discount. All of them, will allow you to drop your profit margin by a certain amount, last one even going into negatives.

The First stage is when you are competing with other stores, say you have an item selling for 19.99, whilst the other store has it for 18.99, so why not lower it? In this case, your profit margin would probably only drop by no more than ten percent.

The second stage is a massive discount, to attract customers – most likely. At this point you can go down with the margin, to even 10%, but you still have to stay profitable.

On the first stage, which has to be your last option, you can go into loss. The only reason this should be used, is to sell out the stock.

Now, let us look a little excel table which will help you out in determining the discount.

	E	F	G	H	I	J	K
4		cost	margin	price	discount margin	discount	discount price
5	p1	$ 34.56	50%	$ 69.12	20%	30% ✓	$ 48.38
6	p2	$ 35.78	50%	$ 71.56	-10%	60%	$ 28.62
7	p3	$ 37.00	40%	$ 61.67	10%	30% ✓	$ 43.17
8	p4	$ 38.22	60%	$ 95.55	10%	50% ✓	$ 47.78
9	p5	$ 29.44	50%	$ 58.88	-10%	60% ✗	$ 23.55
10	p6	$ 10.66	50%	$ 21.32	10%	40% ✗	$ 12.79

H5 function = F5/(100%-G5)

J5 function = (H5-K5)/H5

K5 function = (H5-F5)/(G5/I5)+F5

As you can see, this table allows you to enter your cost, your margin and the desired margin after you add your discount. Once you have this setup, think of the stages and apply those discount margins as you wish.

Important thing to remember is that discounts should start and end, you should have them often, but not every week. If you have too many discount periods, they will mean nothing. Having said that, you should probably have a few items on sale all the time – for those bargain buyers.

PROMOTIONS

You may think that a promotion, is the same as a discount, but it is in fact not true. A discount would be needed for a promotion to happen, but it is a completely different thing. The goal of a promotion is to attract engagement or new potential customers to browse your store.

Any promotion will require a giveaway, so what can it be? A giveaway can be almost everything, including your products and discounts (discount coupons). In case you do not have a lot of stock, you probably do not want to give away your products, therefore you will need to enlist a third-party product. This could be a pen, a pencil, a t-shirt, or if it is more localized, it could be a SPA booking or even a trip. This all depends on the kind of buzz you want to create and how many "winners" you want to have. Now, getting to the discount, you can indeed offer a discount as your promotion item, but it has to be in a form of a coupon.

The next question, is where do you promote? And the obvious answer is – social media, which is a good one. But these days everyone is doing that, so think of some other ways, perhaps you have connections, perhaps you can get your fliers in big venues. Having something tangible will always be better than any social media interaction. For example, if you sell sports items and you have access to sports events. You can buy a few hundred hats, attach a promotional flyer inside it and give them away.

Once you have your location, you need to find the best way to promote. Basically, you have three ways to do it, you can either have a small number of "winners" or a mass amount of "winners", or you can have "everyone wins" arrangement. In this case, a winner is someone who gets that free item, that free coupon or whatever it is you are giving away. This is an important decision and there is no straight way to determine that. But, in case you are doing a contest for one single prize, it must be something worth someone's attention, otherwise you will just look cheap. On the other hand, if you give something to everyone, it has to be something very small and inexpensive, the best thing in that case is a discount coupon.

In general, during any promotion, it is important for the potential customers to engage with your platform, not your Facebook page or other social media outlet. What you want to do, is get them in the store and get them browsing. In a case of a contest, the participation should require a registration to the store. Once you have them in, you will likely get them in the mailing list and you will be able to reach them.

Your first promotions should be very small, just try it, see how it works. It may seem very attractive, but most of the time the results will be disappointing. Do not spend more than hundred dollars on your first one and several next ones after that.

ADVERTISING

Advertising is a vast topic and it is true you can easily get lost in it. But we will try to cover three things – campaigns, budgets and outlets. First, you need to know what kind of campaigns you can have, is it pay-per-click only or is it pay-per-post? Then, you need to know how to budget a campaign or how to budget a budget. Finally, you must find a place to publish your campaign and although it is the last thing to do, it may prove to be the most difficult one.

These days you can find many campaign options and many fancy names for them, but what you should look at is the payment type. Basically, you can have three options – you can pay for clicks, you can pay for views and clicks, or you can do affiliate arrangement where you will pay fixed or percentage-based commission from the sale(s). Obviously, for an online store the most attractive option would be affiliate sale, but the other options might be useful on some specific instances – such as promotions.

When it comes to advertising platforms there are well-known ones and then there are new ones. There is no wrong one, but there are bad ones – do avoid the platforms that serve "cheap" ads on "cheap" websites, unless this is the kind of product you are selling. For more exact guidance you can refer to the following list:

1. LinkedIn – very expensive option, only useful on high-value/high-quality business-oriented products.
2. Facebook – possibly the most popular platform for online stores, flooded with ads from such places and although common option – you should look for something better.
3. Google Ads – they offer search engine ads, website display ads and even video ads (on YouTube). A good option, with reasonable prices, although in terms of search engine – the next option will be cheaper.
4. Microsoft Ads (Bing Ads) – search ads on Microsoft network, relatively easy to use, good cost-per-click rate.

5. Twitter ads – a variety of options, easy to use, the results may be unpredictable.

TIP OF THE SECTION

Diversify your investments, never put your whole budget on one campaign. No matter how good your advertising campaign looks, chances are it will not work, in fact, it is more likely that it will not work than that it will work. If you have five hundred dollars, you have five, hundred dollars, campaigns – not one. Some will work, some will not, but chances are better.

UPKEEP

Staff and other ongoing expenses

STAFF

When it comes to staff you have to be extra careful, most people simply cannot bring themselves to fire people who are no longer useful and then they just add to the cost. In general, for start-up business you do not want any strict contract, any long-term arrangement. You should only pay for what your contractor will do and avoid any kind of hourly arrangement.

OTHER EXPENSES

Any additional expenses will mostly on depend on whether you rent a space or not. If you do, you will first pay rent, then utilities and then some more, so you should account for all of these, because it will be different from doing it all from home.

TIP OF THE SECTION

Never forget, that ongoing expenses are more difficult to cut off. Always think twice before you get on a subscription or hire a new person long-term.

FINANCE

Taxes and general numbers

TAXES

Throughout the book, we have already covered some taxes and how they affect or may affect your plans. Now, we will take a deeper look at the taxes and we will start with the VAT (value added tax).

The VAT tax is interested in a way, that it gets calculated as an addition the sales, not as an expense, not as a cost. For example, if you sell an item for $100 and the cost for that is $50, your gross profit will be $50. However, if you have a VAT tax of 20%, you customer will see a price of $120. The VAT rate is usually included in the price that the customer sees, but the shown price is not the one that is being accounted.

Bellow, you will find a rough example of what your monthly period table should look like. Sales tax is VAT in this case, but it could be something else in other regions.

	period	revenue	sales tax	profit tax	cost	overhead	profit	net profit (bt)	net profit (at)

Table (columns E–Q, rows 4–12):

E	F	G	H	I	J	K	L	M	N	O	P	Q
period	1	2	3	4	5	6	7	8	9	10	11	12
revenue	10000	13000	16000	19000	22000	25000	28000	31000	34000	37000	40000	43000
sales tax	2100	2730	3360	3990	4620	5250	5880	6510	7140	7770	8400	9030
profit tax	450	675	900	1125	1350	1575	1800	1725	1950	2175	2400	2625
cost	5000	6500	8000	9500	11000	12500	14000	15500	17000	18500	20000	21500
overhead	2000	2000	2000	2000	2000	2000	2000	4000	4000	4000	4000	4000
profit	5000	6500	8000	9500	11000	12500	14000	15500	17000	18500	20000	21500
net profit (bt)	3000	4500	6000	7500	9000	10500	12000	11500	13000	14500	16000	17500
net profit (at)	2550	3825	5100	6375	7650	8925	10200	9775	11050	12325	13600	14875

	B	C
4	vat	21%
5	profit tax	15%

F6 function = F5*C4   *drag right*

F7 function = F11*C5   *drag right*

F10 function = F5–F8   *drag right*

F11 function = F5–F8–F9   *drag right*

F12 function = F11–F7   *drag right*

As you can see, you get all the major statistics for the whole   year.

PUTTING THINGS TOGETHER

Once you have all the details of your plan, you will need to connect everything. The best way to do, is to go in sequence in which you started planning. But, more importantly you need to know your final budget and make final adjustments if something exceeds it.

We will create an excel book, which will contain all budget plans and bring them to one single sheet.

	E	F	G	H	I
4	period	1	2	3	4
5	revenue	$ -	$ 4,285.71	$ 5,357.14	$ 5,785.71
6	marketing expenses	$ -	$ 2,000.00	$ 2,500.00	$ 2,700.00
7	stock expenses	$ 4,000.00	$ 1,250.00	$ 2,700.00	$ 3,100.00
8	staff expenses	$ 1,180.00	$ 350.00	$ 310.00	$ 330.00
9	other expenses	$ 1,852.00	$ 922.00	$ 922.00	$ 922.00
10	total expenses	$ 7,032.00	$ 4,522.00	$ 6,432.00	$ 7,052.00
11	net profit	$ (5,977.20)	$ (236.29)	$ (1,074.86)	$ (1,266.29)

Final 1

	J	K	L	M	N
4	5	6	7	8	9
5	$ 6,214.29	$ 6,642.86	$ 7,071.43	$ 7,500.00	$ 7,500.00
6	$ 2,900.00	$ 3,100.00	$ 3,300.00	$ 3,500.00	$ 3,500.00
7	$ 3,300.00	$ 3,500.00	$ 3,700.00	$ 3,700.00	
8	$ 410.00	$ 550.00	$ 1,080.00	$ 1,080.00	$ 1,680.00
9	$ 932.00	$ 956.00	$ 986.00	$ 996.00	$ 1,006.00
10	$ 7,542.00	$ 8,106.00	$ 9,066.00	$ 9,276.00	$ 6,186.00
11	$ (1,327.71)	$ (1,463.14)	$ (1,994.57)	$ (1,776.00)	$ 1,314.00

Final 2

	O	P	Q
4	10	11	12
5	$ 7,500.00	$ 7,500.00	$ 7,500.00
6	$ 3,500.00	$ 3,500.00	$ 3,500.00
7			
8	$ 1,680.00	$ 1,680.00	$ 1,680.00
9	$ 1,016.00	$ 1,026.00	$ 1,036.00
10	$ 6,196.00	$ 6,206.00	$ 6,216.00
11	$ 1,304.00	$ 1,294.00	$ 1,284.00

Final 3

First we have a sheet (Final 1,Final 2,Final 3) contains one table, which in turn contains the projections for 12 periods in all different sections. Do note that values in brackets are negative. After that, we will have sheets for different sections.

	A	B	C	D	E	F	G
1	employee	cost		expenses		employee	cost		expenses
2	accountan	$ 250.00	$ 30.00		accountan	$ 250.00	$ -
3	developer	$ 700.00	$ -		designer	$ 100.00	$ -
4	seo specia	$ 200.00	$ -		sub total	$ 350.00	$ -
5	sub total	$ 1,150.00	$ 30.00		total	$	350.00
6	total	$	1,180.00				

Final 4

	I	J	K	L	M	N	O
1	employee	cost		expenses		employee	cost		expenses
2	accountan	$ 250.00	$ -		accountan	$ 250.00	$ -
3	designer	$ 60.00	$ -		designer	$ 80.00	$ -
4	sub total	$ 310.00	$ -		sub total	$ 330.00	$ -
5	total	$	310.00		total	$	330.00

Final 5

	A	B	C	D	E	F	G
9	employee	cost		expenses		employee	cost		expenses
10	accountan	$ 250.00	$ -		accountan	$ 250.00	$ -
11	designer	$ 160.00	$ -		administra	$ 300.00	$ -
12	sub total	$ 410.00	$ -		sub total	$ 550.00	$ -
13	total	$	410.00		total	$	550.00

Final 6

	I	J	K	L	M	N	O
9	employee	cost		expenses		employee	cost		expenses
10	accountan	$ 250.00	$ -		accountan	$ 250.00	$ -
11	designer	$ 200.00			designer	$ 200.00	
12	administra	$ 300.00	$ -		administra	$ 300.00	$ -
13	customer	$ 300.00	$ 30.00		customer	$ 300.00	$ 30.00
14	sub total	$ 1,050.00	$ 30.00		sub total	$ 1,050.00	$ 30.00
15	total	$	1,080.00		total	$	1,080.00

Final 7

	A	B	C	D	E	F	G
18	employee	cost	expenses		employee	cost	expenses
19	accountan	$ 250.00	$ -		accountan	$ 250.00	$ -
20	designer	$ 200.00			designer	$ 200.00	
21	administra	$ 900.00	$ -		administra	$ 900.00	$ -
22	customer	$ 300.00	$ 30.00		customer	$ 300.00	$ 30.00
23	sub total	$ 1,650.00	$ 30.00		sub total	$ 1,650.00	$ 30.00
24	total	$	1,680.00		total	$	1,680.00

Final 8

	A	B	C	D	E	F	G
18	employee	cost	expenses		employee	cost	expenses
19	accountan	$ 250.00	$ -		accountan	$ 250.00	$ -
20	designer	$ 200.00			designer	$ 200.00	
21	administra	$ 900.00	$ -		administra	$ 900.00	$ -
22	customer	$ 300.00	$ 30.00		customer	$ 300.00	$ 30.00
23	sub total	$ 1,650.00	$ 30.00		sub total	$ 1,650.00	$ 30.00
24	total	$	1,680.00		total	$	1,680.00

Final 9

The sheet "staff" (Final 4,Final 5,Final 6,Final 7,Final 8,Final 9) contains twelve tables for each period. Since the staff you have for each period will change, you need to be flexible with your tables.

	B	C	D	E
5	rent	$ 800.00	$ 800.00	$ 800.00
6	phone	$ 40.00	$ 40.00	$ 40.00
7	electricity	$ 35.00	$ 35.00	$ 35.00
8	internet	$ 15.00	$ 15.00	$ 15.00
9	hosting	$ 12.00	$ 12.00	$ 12.00
10	furniture	$ 500.00		
11	other	$ 450.00	$ 20.00	$ 20.00
12	total	$ 1,852.00	$ 922.00	$ 922.00

Final 10

	F	G	H	I	J
5	$ 800.00	$ 800.00	$ 800.00	$ 800.00	$ 800.00
6	$ 40.00	$ 40.00	$ 40.00	$ 70.00	$ 70.00
7	$ 35.00	$ 35.00	$ 35.00	$ 35.00	$ 35.00
8	$ 15.00	$ 15.00	$ 15.00	$ 15.00	$ 15.00
9	$ 12.00	$ 22.00	$ 36.00	$ 36.00	$ 36.00
10					
11	$ 20.00	$ 20.00	$ 30.00	$ 30.00	$ 40.00
12	$ 922.00	$ 932.00	$ 956.00	$ 986.00	$ 996.00

Final 11

	K	L	M	N
5	$ 800.00	$ 800.00	$ 800.00	$ 800.00
6	$ 70.00	$ 70.00	$ 70.00	$ 70.00
7	$ 35.00	$ 35.00	$ 35.00	$ 35.00
8	$ 15.00	$ 15.00	$ 15.00	$ 15.00
9	$ 36.00	$ 36.00	$ 36.00	$ 36.00
10				
11	$ 50.00	$ 60.00	$ 70.00	$ 80.00
12	$ 1,006.00	$ 1,016.00	$ 1,026.00	$ 1,036.00

Final 12

Other expenses sheet (Final 10,Final 11,Final 12) will contain any expenses that do not fit in other categories.

	D	E	F	G
	period	period budget	number of campaigns	budget per campaign
4	period	period budget	number of campaigns	budget per campaign
5	1	$ -	1	$ -
6	2	$ 2,000.00	15	$ 133.33
7	3	$ 2,500.00	14	$ 178.57
8	4	$ 2,700.00	15	$ 180.00
9	5	$ 2,900.00	16	$ 181.25
10	6	$ 3,100.00	17	$ 182.35
11	7	$ 3,300.00	18	$ 183.33
12	8	$ 3,500.00	19	$ 184.21
13	9	$ 3,500.00	20	$ 175.00
14	10	$ 3,500.00	21	$ 166.67
15	11	$ 3,500.00	22	$ 159.09
16	12	$ 3,500.00	23	$ 152.17

Final 13

	J	K	L	M	N	O	P	Q
4	period	budget	cpc	clicks	conversion	avarege pu	campaign revenue	campaign profit
5	1	$ -	$ 0.35	0	3%	$ 25.00	$ -	$ -
6	2	$ 133.33	$ 0.35	381	3%	$ 25.00	$ 285.71	$ 152.38
7	3	$ 178.57	$ 0.35	510	3%	$ 25.00	$ 382.65	$ 204.08
8	4	$ 180.00	$ 0.35	514	3%	$ 25.00	$ 385.71	$ 205.71
9	5	$ 181.25	$ 0.35	518	3%	$ 25.00	$ 388.39	$ 207.14
10	6	$ 182.35	$ 0.35	521	3%	$ 25.00	$ 390.76	$ 208.40
11	7	$ 183.33	$ 0.35	524	3%	$ 25.00	$ 392.86	$ 209.52
12	8	$ 184.21	$ 0.35	526	3%	$ 25.00	$ 394.74	$ 210.53
13	9	$ 175.00	$ 0.35	500	3%	$ 25.00	$ 375.00	$ 200.00
14	10	$ 166.67	$ 0.35	476	3%	$ 25.00	$ 357.14	$ 190.48
15	11	$ 159.09	$ 0.35	455	3%	$ 25.00	$ 340.91	$ 181.82
16	12	$ 152.17	$ 0.35	435	3%	$ 25.00	$ 326.09	$ 173.91

Final 14

Finally, you can see the table representing your advertisement campaigns plan for the next 12 periods (months). This is very important, because it will be the only way to predict earnings for those initial periods.

TIP OF THE COURSE

No matter what you choose to do and which direction you choose to go – the important thing is to plan ahead and keep your budget tight.

FOR YOUR REFERENCE

Watch the related course on Udemy:
https://www.udemy.com/course/establish-business-strategy-for-an-online-store/?referralCode=F3E991876479CF26040D

Want to become a developer? Start here with C# language for free:
https://learncsharp.conficienssolutio.com

www.ingramcontent.com/pod-product-compliance
Lightning Source LLC
Chambersburg PA
CBHW021511210526
45463CB00002B/980